SHAKTI GAWAIN

THE FOUR
LEVELS *of*
HEALING

A guide to balancing
the spiritual, mental, emotional,
and physical aspects of life

MJF BOOKS
NEW YORK

The author of this book does not despense medical advice, or prescribe the use of any technique as a form of treatment for physical or medical problems without the advice of a physician, either directly or indirectly. The intent of the author is onlly to offer information of a general nature to help you in your quest for emotional well-being and good health. In the event you use any of the information in this book for yourself, which is your constitutional right, the author and the publisher assume no responsibility for your actions.

Published by MJF Books
Fine Communications
Two Lincoln Square
60 West 66th Street
New York, NY 10023

The Four Levels of Healing
Library of Congress Control No. 2001119127
ISBN 1-56731-496-1

Edited by Kathryn Altman

This edition published by arrangement with New World Library.

Manufactured in the United States of America on acid-free paper ∞

MJF Books and the MJF colophon are trademarks of Fine Creative Media, Inc.

BG   10 9   8   7   6   5   4   3   2   1

To Kathy, for all the years of loving friendship, guidance, support, and creative inspiration.

TABLE OF CONTENTS

ACKNOWLEDGMENTS

I thank Kathy Altman for nudging me to write this book and for contributing wonderful ideas, suggestions, feedback, and editing.

Thanks to my mother, Beth Gawain, for your helpful comments.

Mary Brewer, I appreciate your dedicated typing and retyping, late into the night.

Thank you, Lora O'Connor, for doing just about everything else to shape this book and get it out there.

And thanks to my sweetheart, Jim, for your loving support and help.

Introduction

We are living in a profoundly exciting and challenging time. Humanity as a whole, and each of us as individuals, are confronted with the fact that the ways we have been accustomed to living no longer work for us, or our planet.

As we wake up to this, many of us realize we are involved in a difficult, yet fascinating learning process — our own personal evolution and the evolution of human consciousness.

We can no longer follow the paths to which we are accustomed. The materialistic approach to life leaves us spiritually empty and emotionally unfulfilled, and is rapidly destroying the earth. The spiritual philosophies of both the Eastern and Western traditions no longer work for many of us; they deny too much of our human experience — the physical and emotional aspects of our being. And our intense cultural focus on intellectual and technological development has left our entire world dangerously out of balance.

For our own personal satisfaction, we need to find ways to develop and express all aspects of who we are. And for the common good, we have to find a way to live on earth with greater consciousness.

In order to do this, we need to look honestly at ourselves, to recognize the areas of unconsciousness in our lives. We must learn how to heal the wounded places within us and nurture our own growth and development.

Many of us are searching for insight, practical guidance, and tools that can support us in this process.

It has helped me greatly to understand that there are four very different aspects of life — the spiritual, mental, emotional, and physical. Each of these areas needs to be healed and developed in specific, and sometimes very different, ways.

I created this book in response to the many requests for a written work on this topic from people who have attended my workshops and lectures and heard me discuss the four levels of existence.

Much of the material is drawn from my audiotape of the same name and from my book *The Path of Transformation: How Healing Ourselves Can Change the World*. I have also included quite a bit of material here not found in any of my other books or tapes.

The journey of consciousness is not easy, but it is the most vital and rewarding thing we can do. I hope this book will help you in the ongoing process of developing and balancing all aspects of your life.

With love,
Shakti Gawain

THE FOUR
LEVELS *of*
HEALING

~

CHAPTER 1

THE FOUR LEVELS OF EXISTENCE

Human life consists of four aspects: the spiritual, mental, emotional, and physical levels of existence. In order to find balance, wholeness, and fulfillment in our lives, we need to heal, develop, and integrate all four of these aspects within ourselves.

Our spiritual aspect is our inner essence, our soul, the part of us that exists beyond time and space. It connects us with the universal source and the oneness of all life. Developing our awareness of the spiritual level of our being allows us to experience a feeling of belonging in the universe, a deeper meaning and purpose in our lives, and a broader perspective than we have from our personality alone. The spiritual level provides a foundation for the development of the other levels.

Our mental aspect is our intellect, our ability to think and reason. The mental level of our existence consists of our thoughts, attitudes, beliefs, and values. Our minds can be our greatest gift, and at times, our greatest curse. They can cause us terrible confusion or bring us profound understanding. Developing the mental level of our being allows us to think clearly, remain open minded, yet discriminate intelligently. Our minds enable us to gather knowledge and wisdom from our life experience and from the world around us.

Our emotional aspect is our ability to experience life deeply, to relate to one another and the world on a feeling level. It's the part of us that seeks meaningful contact and connection with others. Developing the emotional level of our being allows us to feel the full range of the human experience, and find fulfillment in our relationships with ourselves and each other.

Our physical aspect is, of course, our physical body. It also includes our ability to survive and thrive in the material world. Developing the physical level of our being involves learning to take good care of our bodies, and to enjoy them. It also means developing the skills to live comfortably and effectively in the world.

All four of these levels of existence are equally important. In the long run, we can't afford to neglect any of them. If we want to feel whole and lead healthy, satisfying lives, we need to focus a certain amount of time and attention on healing and developing each aspect.

Most of us have had the opportunity to develop certain parts of ourselves more than others. Maybe we were actively discouraged from expressing certain aspects, or we simply did not know how.

Some levels may need special healing because we were wounded or suffered trauma in that area. For example, if you were taught certain spiritual beliefs you eventually felt weren't right for you, and as a result rejected the entire spiritual side of life, you may have a wound on the spiritual level, which can be healed by developing your own personal way of relating to spirit. If you don't feel confident intellectually, you may have a wound on the mental level. All of us have suffered some degree of disappointment, hurt, or pain that leaves us emotionally wounded and in need of healing. Many of us have certain physical weaknesses that need special attention. We may lack the confidence to live successfully in the material world, in which case we can heal ourselves by developing certain skills.

There's no one right way to carry out our healing process. Everyone is different and follows a unique path of development. We may proceed in developing the four levels in any order, or all at once. Our lives definitely guide us in this process.

For example, I was born into a very intellectual and educated family in which the mental aspect of life was highly valued. So, I developed the mental level of my being early in life. I was a good student and an avid reader. My parents were atheists, so I had very little experience with the spiritual aspect of life. Because I was not brought up with any religious beliefs or dogma, I began searching for the deeper meaning and purpose in my life, which led me to read and study psychology and philosophy.

In college, I became aware of the fact that I was out of balance by being much too intellectual. The only class I really enjoyed was my dance class, which allowed me to get out of my head and experience my body. Eventually, I transferred to another college and majored in dance. I also began practicing hatha yoga regularly. This was a period of intense focus on developing the physical aspect of my being.

Eventually, my quest for consciousness led me to study meditation, travel through India and around the world, read many metaphysical books, and attend many personal growth workshops. During this time I focused primarily on developing the spiritual aspect of my life, reconnecting with my soul, and developing my ability to trust and follow my inner intuitive guidance. In this period I wrote my first two books, *Creative Visualization* and *Living in the Light*.

After a few years of wonderful success in my work, I began to recognize that there was a great deal of unhappiness in my life in the area of relationships. I yearned for more consistent closeness and intimacy in all my relationships, and I was particularly longing to find the right man to share my life with. This led me into a period of several years in which I focused on my deep emotional healing, getting in touch with and releasing old self-defeating patterns, and developing my ability to give and receive love in a healthier way. I'm happy to report I now have a great deal of intimacy in my life, and I am married to a wonderful, loving man (but that is a story for another book!).

Currently in my life, I work on all four levels. At times I need to focus on one more than the others, but generally I work on greater balance and integration of them all. I make a daily practice of listening to and following my inner spiritual guidance, and my work brings me continual mental challenge and stimulation. I go to therapy from time to time to work on deeper levels of emotional healing, and I try to maintain a regular routine of physical exercise, outdoor time, healthy eating, and massage.

Each of us has our own unique path on this journey, and our own way of proceeding. We are all on an evolutionary journey, but most of us don't realize it until a certain period of awakening, when we begin to realize that life is a school, and we are all involved in the process of growth and learning.

That awakening may happen on any or all of the four levels. One person might have a spontaneous mystical experience, or a near-death experience, that opens her to begin exploring the spiritual realm of existence. Another person might be drawn into the healing process on an emotional level; perhaps because of a divorce or other crisis, he seeks counseling and begins gaining insight and awareness about the emotional aspect of his being. Still another person might "wake up" on the mental level, while reading a particularly fascinating book. Many people begin their awakening process on a physical level, because of a health crisis, an addiction problem, or simply a desire to learn to live in a healthier, more harmonious way. So the conscious personal growth process can start at any level.

Once we've developed one aspect, life moves us to explore another aspect. At times we may be working on two or three or all four levels at once. The four levels are interrelated and any work we do on one affects all the others.

Many of us are drawn primarily to one or two of the four levels, and tend to focus most of our attention there. For example, an acquaintance of mine is a professional athlete whose main focus is on her physical development. A mechanic friend of mine happens to be a gourmet cook who absolutely loves good food. His attention is also primarily on the physical plane.

My father was the classic absentminded professor. Most of the time his attention was focused on a very abstract mental plane, to the point where he could easily forget about his own physical needs and surroundings.

I know several people who are very drawn to a quiet, contemplative lifestyle; the spiritual aspect of life is their area of primary development.

My friend Judy is a devoted wife and mother who focuses most of her attention on nurturing her family (emotional level) and managing her household (physical level) and feels very fulfilled by these activities.

A successful businessman I know seems to spend all his time and energy on running his business and making money, which requires a combination of his mental and physical aspects.

Some people have a destiny to strongly develop only one or two levels. We all have certain areas of greater development, but most of us, in order to find real fulfillment, *do* need to develop and balance all the levels, at least to some degree. Otherwise, we eventually experience a certain emptiness, stuckness, frustration, or longing.

For example, if we have done a great deal of spiritual and mental development but ignored the emotional and physical levels, we might have wonderful ideas and magnificent visions but have a hard time making a living, difficulty making relationships work, or problems with our health. A person who is very physically developed but has not developed the emotional and mental levels may be strong and healthy, but have difficulty expressing his thoughts and feelings.

So for our own personal satisfaction and fulfillment, it is important to look at the areas of our lives in which we may be out of balance, and take steps to develop the aspects of ourselves we haven't yet explored or fully expressed.

Bringing Healing and Balance Into the World

It is also important to look on a collective level at how our culture and our world are out of balance. Our modern western culture has focused intensely on developing the mental and physical levels. As a result, we have amazing technology and have made many incredible advances on the physical plane. However, we have largely disowned the spiritual and emotional levels. As a result, our entire world is dangerously out of balance, and we are experiencing tremendous difficulties on all levels.

Spiritually, our culture is largely disconnected from a sense of meaning and purpose. We have lost our connection to nature and our sense of interrelatedness with all beings. This spiritual emptiness is at the core of most of our social, political, and environmental crises.

Mentally, the old ideas, beliefs, and values we still hold are no longer serving us. Many of the governmental, economic, and religious systems we believe in and live by are breaking down or no longer working. Our obsession with technology, while productive in many ways, has carried us away from our hearts and souls.

Emotionally, we have lost our sense of family and community, and our feeling of belonging somewhere. We have severe social and emotional crises, including alcoholism, drug addiction, depression, alienation, and violence.

Physically, our planet is over-populated and polluted, and our natural resources are being rapidly consumed and destroyed.

Since we are all part of the collective consciousness of humanity, any healing work we do individually is transmitted into the mass consciousness. So every evolutionary step we take in our own growth process contributes to the evolution of humanity. Clearly then, it is important to do the work of developing and balancing the four levels, not only for our own personal satisfaction, but also as a contribution to healing our planet.

As you do this work, keep in mind that all four levels of life are closely related to, and affected by, one another. As we heal one level, we support the development of all the other levels. Strengthening our spiritual connection gives us the inspiration and courage we need to face deep emotional healing. As we do our emotional healing work we release blocked energies, thereby clearing the mental and physical levels as well. The more in tune we are with our physical bodies, the more energy we feel on every level.

We may begin the process on any of the levels, and explore the various realms at different times in our lives. The ultimate goal is the integration of them all by developing and balancing ourselves — spiritually, mentally, emotionally, and physically. As we do this, not only do we bring harmony and wholeness into our own lives, we also help to bring healing and balance to the world.

Exercise: Assessing the Four Levels

Take a few minutes to think about which of the four aspects you have developed and which one(s) might need more healing and expression in your life.

Physical: Are you physically healthy and active? Do you like and feel comfortable in your body? Do you enjoy your sexuality? Are you comfortable in the material world? Are you practical, down-to-earth, financially stable?

Emotional: Are you in touch with your feelings and able to express them appropriately? Do you allow yourself to feel the full range of emotions — fear, sadness, anger, as well as love and joy — or do you find that certain emotions make you uncomfortable? Are you able to set appropriate boundaries with people? Can you relate to others in a close, intimate way?

Mental: Are you satisfied with your intellect? Can you think and express yourself clearly? Do you have a belief system that supports you and works for you? Are you open to new ideas without being overly impressionable?

Spiritual: Do you feel a sense of connection to your spiritual source? Are you able to spend time quiet and alone, just being? Do you have a relationship with your own inner wisdom or intuitive guidance? Do you have moments when you feel at one with everything or part of some greater whole?

You might find one or two of these areas stand out as needing your attention, or you may feel that all four aspects need a little tuning up. Perhaps you will find that you are already very developed and balanced on all levels.

If you wish, write out the answers to the previous questions and write about how you experience each of the four levels in your life at this time. Note any ideas you have about steps you can take toward greater development and balance. Also, take notice of any resistance that comes up about any of the levels.

CHAPTER 2

~

HEALING
THE
SPIRITUAL LEVEL

Many of us in the modern western world feel profoundly disconnected from our spiritual source. Our culture, in its pursuit of intellectual and physical development, seems to have lost track of the spiritual dimension of life.

As individuals, when we are disconnected from our own essential being and the universal spirit, we feel empty, lost, and alone. We lose our feeling of belonging in the universe. Our lives lack the sense of meaning and purpose they should rightly have.

Unconsciously, we strive to fill this inner void in many ways. We may be driven to seek money, power, or success, or search for the perfect relationship to bring us happiness and fulfillment. We may fall into addictive behaviors, using food, alcohol, drugs, work, compulsive sex, shopping, or gambling as a way to try to fill ourselves up and avoid our pain. Sooner or later, we discover that none of these methods can fill an emptiness that is fundamentally spiritual.

As I mentioned in the previous chapter, this lack of connection to spirit is the root of many of our social and cultural ills, as well as our personal problems. As a culture we feel and behave as if we are alone on this earth, unrelated to those who lived before us, those who will come after us, and even those other cultures and other species currently sharing the planet with us. Addiction, violence, and our other social ailments are symptoms of deep spiritual and emotional alienation.

These problems in our world are a reflection of the personal conflicts and issues we are all dealing with. Since the collective consciousness is made up of individuals, these collective problems can only be truly resolved when we, as individuals, take responsibility for healing ourselves on the deepest levels. We can't expect to find meaningful and effective solutions to our social problems if we aren't willing or able to do our own personal healing work. Doing our own consciousness work is very challenging; sometimes it may seem easier to try addressing seemingly external problems with external solutions. While these steps may be part of the process of resolution, true and lasting healing can only come from deep within.

I've addressed healing ourselves on the spiritual level first, because it is the foundation of our healing process. Spiritual healing occurs as we find a way to consciously reconnect with our essential being — the wise, loving, powerful, creative entity we are at our core.

Through this connection with our spiritual essence, we begin to re-experience our oneness with all other beings and all of nature. The more we connect with this essential oneness, the more we experience a sense of safety, trust, and fulfillment — a feeling of belonging where we are. Rather than thirsting for wholeness and trying to fill it from the outside, we experience our inner emptiness being filled from a source within.

This contact with our spiritual dimension gives us an expanded perspective on our lives, both as individuals and part of humanity. Rather than just being caught up in the daily frustrations and struggles of our personality, we can see things from the perspective of the soul. We are able to look at the bigger picture of our life here on Earth, which helps us understand much more about why we are here and what we are doing; It helps us put our daily problems in a larger perspective, and find the deeper meaning and purpose in our lives.

Developing our spiritual awareness gives us a foundation from which we can more easily move into the other levels of healing. Without the ability to make this inner spiritual connection, it may be very difficult or even impossible to find the inspiration, understanding, and strength we need to confront the difficulties and challenges of healing the other levels.

How does spiritual healing take place? For some people it begins quite suddenly and surprisingly with some type of spontaneous mystical experience, such as a near-death experience, a vision, or a powerful dream. A spiritual awakening often takes place at a time of great physical or emotional crisis, when the more superficial preoccupations of life fall away and leave one with an experience of the profound. Many people dealing with addiction find that their connection to a higher power comes initially through sheer desperation. Frequently, people get in touch with the spiritual dimension through an illness of their own or a loved one. The birth of a baby can sometimes be the catalyst for parents to experience a profound opening to the miraculous. Simply finding oneself in a place and time of peace, quiet, and retreat can sometimes trigger a spiritual experience.

For many of us, spiritual awakening does not take place suddenly or spontaneously, but is something we long for and cultivate deliberately through a spiritual practice such as regular meditation or prayer. Our spiritual connection may develop slowly and gradually over many years.

Throughout history, human beings have often used one type of consciousness-altering substance or another as a way to access the spiritual dimension. In my generation, many people found an initial spiritual opening through the use of marijuana, LSD, and other mind-altering drugs. While drug use can be a very powerful and effective way to open up the spiritual level of our being, it is, of course, fraught with danger. While a drug may initially help one find the path to an expanded consciousness, the real challenge is to find that path again and again, without relying on external help. Unfortunately, it is extremely tempting for many to keep using the drug as a crutch, which leads to dependency and addiction, eventually resulting in further soul loss, rather than soul retrieval.

How do we best cultivate our spiritual healing and development? Through any activity or experience that nurtures our soul. We must begin to pay attention to discovering what feeds us in this way.

Whenever we can bring our attention, awareness, and energy into the moment to be fully present with ourselves, we begin to tap into the spiritual dimension, in which we experience a feeling of connection, oneness, and flow. Whatever we do wholeheartedly will nurture us spiritually.

Our western culture places great value on doing. We are taught that we should be as active, focused, and productive as possible. Most of us feel guilty when we are not engaged in some type of productive activity, either physically or mentally. We fear that we are wasting our precious time if we are not obviously accomplishing something tangible.

If and when we do relax, we often feel that we must be constantly entertained, or must fill up the time and space with radio, television, or other distractions.

Very little value is placed on the experience of simply being. It is seen as a lack of something, rather an important energy in itself. Yet being is as important as doing. Our lack of understanding of this is the root of many of our greatest problems.

Being time allows us to rest and recharge. It allows us to take our focus off the outside world and move inward, where we can make contact with ourselves. The ability to simply be quiet for a while is the doorway to our deeper dimensions; it is necessary to enter the realm of being in order to deeply connect with the spirit.

We bring spiritual healing into our lives when we find a way to make regular contact with these deeper aspects of ourselves. This means developing some type of spiritual practice that works for us, then making a commitment to doing it on a regular basis.

Finding a Spiritual Practice

For some people, a spiritual practice might involve a time of silent meditation, either alone or in a group. It might include attending church services or some other type of inspirational activity. However, a spiritual practice does not have to be religious in any traditional sense. It can be any activity or ritual that helps us to experience our spiritual essence, even if only briefly.

A great number of people find their spiritual connection primarily through contact with nature. Often times, people are not fully conscious of this. They just know that they love being outdoors, that they feel exhilarated, peaceful, or high from the experience. Many find themselves drawn to a particular outdoor activity and feel enlivened by it in some way that goes deeper than simply the physical and emotional enjoyment of the experience.

The natural world is filled with the life force. The less disturbed or developed the area, the more powerful the energy there. Spending time in a natural environment supports and reinforces our connection to our own inner nature. So if you live in a city, a simple stroll in the park can be a spiritual renewal. A walk in the woods, a hike in the mountains, sitting quietly on a rock by a river, and swimming in or simply watching the ocean can all be profound moments of spiritual healing.

Quite often when we go out to enjoy nature, we go with a friend or a group and we chat the entire time. While fun and rewarding in other ways (perhaps fulfilling our needs on the emotional and mental levels), this can cause us to miss out on the spiritual aspect of the experience. So if you are drawn to being in nature as a spiritual practice, consider going alone sometimes. Even when you go with others, you may want to take a little time to be alone and quiet, or suggest that everyone enjoy a period of silence together.

Although we often equate spiritual practice with silence and stillness, it can be found in movement too. In fact, many people find their spiritual connection primarily through physical activity, such as running, bicycling, or dancing. If you are a very mentally or physically active person who has a hard time slowing down or relaxing enough to practice sitting meditation, by all means, try moving meditation. One of the best forms of moving meditation I know is the one taught by Gabrielle Roth in her work with the five rhythms of life. These five rhythms form a wave pattern — starting with Flowing, building to Staccato, peaking in Chaos, lightening up in Lyrical, and finding a quiet place inside in Stillness. (For more information about Gabrielle's work, see the Recommended Resources section at the end of this book.)

Find a physical activity you enjoy and fully pour your energy and attention into it. At a certain point, you may find yourself feeling in the flow, being moved by a higher force, feeling at one with life, or you may have an experience of great peace, inspiration, or clarity. You may find that after a period of all-out physical activity, you are then able to relax and move into quiet meditation.

Another form of spiritual practice is through creative expression. Many people find a deep connection with themselves through drawing, painting, sculpting, making pottery, writing, singing, making music, or dancing. If you find yourself yearning toward one of these forms of expression, give yourself a chance to explore it. Keep in mind that you are doing this for your own fulfillment and satisfaction, so it doesn't matter whether you are good at it from the point of view of any external standard or comparison. Give yourself permission to keep this activity totally private if this makes it more comfortable for you. Three excellent resources for support in creative practice are Hal Bennett's book *Write from the Heart*, Julia Cameron's *The Artist's Way*, and *Life, Paint and Passion*, by Michell Cassou and Stewart Cubley.

Actually, anything we do can be a spiritual practice, if we focus our attention on it in such a way that we become fully present and connected with ourselves. Cleaning house, washing dishes, shoveling snow, walking the dog, or any other daily activity can be a deeply peaceful or exhilarating experience if we use it as a practice for staying in the present moment.

Here are a few other suggestions for daily or weekly rituals that can become part of your spiritual practice:

- Check in with yourself and ask for inner guidance for a few minutes when you first wake up and at other moments during the day.

- Begin or end your day with a few minutes of yoga, tai chi, or another physical and spiritual discipline.

- Spend a few moments in prayer or silent gratitude before meals.

- Take a cool invigorating shower at the beginning of the day.

- Soak in a hot bath by candlelight at the end of the day.

- Water your garden or your plants with the

mindfulness that you give physical nourishment to them, and they give beauty and spiritual nourishment back to you.

A friend of mine takes a day of silence each week. Everyone knows this is his day of rest, to rest his voice, his mind, and his body, and to listen deeply to himself. If a full day is not possible for you, you can start with an hour or two, one day or evening a week, when you can simply be alone with a quiet mind and no outside distractions — no phone, no television, no visitors, no family responsibilities.

Another acquaintance of mine doesn't have any organized religious affiliations, but keeps her time unscheduled on Sundays to listen to her own needs and be spontaneous. Freeing herself from obligations and plans this way allows her to renew her inner self and provides a balance to her busy schedule during the week.

A musician I know takes a moment before he practices his music each day to thank his spiritual source for the gift of his voice and the ability to make music.

For me, the most important spiritual practice has been developing the daily habit of tuning into my intuitive inner guidance and learning to trust and act on it, moment by moment in my life. For a more complete explanation of this practice, please see my book *Living in the Light*, listed in Recommended Resources.

Some people use oracles such as the *I Ching* or the *Tarot* to remind them of and reflect their own inner wisdom. Whatever works for you is great! Just make certain that you have some form of spiritual renewal and inspiration as a regular part of your life. A regular spiritual practice is healing and nourishing to all levels of our being — the body, emotions, and mind, as well as the soul.

Exercise: Spiritual Guidance Meditation

Meditation is a way of taking time to become aware of our thoughts, feelings, and bodily sensations, thus allowing us to reach a deeper level in which we can touch our spiritual essence. Here's a simple meditation that you can adopt as a regular spiritual practice if you like. I suggest that you read through the entire meditation before you begin.

First, find a spot to designate as your place of spiritual retreat. Choose a place in or near your home so you have regular, easy access to it. It's wonderful if this place is outdoors with some natural beauty surrounding it, but most important, it should be quiet, peaceful, and comfortable. It could be a spot in your backyard, a special room in your house, or a corner of a room. Make it unique by designating a certain chair, pillow, or blanket that you only use while meditating. Make sure you will be uninterrupted for at least fifteen minutes, or longer if possible.

Find a comfortable position either sitting or lying down. If you're lying down, it's best to lie flat on your back, perhaps with a pillow under your knees if that makes it more comfortable for you. If you're sitting, sit with your back as straight as possible, supported by the back of your chair, with your feet flat on the floor. Having your spine straight and your body comfortably supported makes it much easier for your body to deeply relax and for the energy to flow through you freely.

Once you're comfortable, close your eyes and begin to relax. Take a few deep breaths, filling your lungs with air. As you slowly exhale, think of relaxing your entire body.

Take a few more deep breaths and as you exhale, relax your body as deeply and as completely as you can. Let yourself focus for a few minutes on breathing in and relaxing as you exhale.

Let your awareness move through your body from your head to your toes, and notice if there's any place in your body that feels tight or tense. If so, put your attention on that area, take a deep breath, and as you slowly exhale, imagine all the tightness, tension, or excess energy draining out of your body. Imagine that area releasing and relaxing. Take another deep breath, and as you exhale, imagine your whole body deeply relaxed and the energy flowing through freely.

Now, take another deep breath and as you exhale, relax your mind. Let your thoughts float away, like clouds in the sky. As each new thought comes up in your mind, notice it and let it go. Let it float away like a cloud. When the next thought comes, notice that, then let that one go, too. As soon as you notice yourself having a thought, let it go and let it become a cloud floating away in the blue sky. There's nothing you need to hold onto mentally right now. You can just let it all go. Let your mind slow down and become very quiet and calm, like the water in a still lake or pond, so peaceful there's not even a ripple on the surface. Remember to keep relaxing your body and breathing deeply.

Take another deep breath and as you exhale, let your awareness begin to move deep within. With every breath, as you exhale, let yourself move a little deeper, until you come to rest in the quietest place you can find inside of you, deep within the core of your being. Then just let yourself rest in this quiet place where there's nothing you have to do, nowhere you have to go — just being quiet.

Each one of us naturally has a connection to our own spiritual essence. We can get in touch with the wisdom of our spirit in this deep place inside. It is not something separate from ourselves, it is just the deepest part of who we are.

When you feel ready, ask if your spirit has any message it wants to give you, anything it wants to remind you of, or make you aware of. Then just sit quietly. Notice if any thought, feeling, or image comes to you in response to this question. Trust whatever comes, if it feels right to you. Take your time; don't worry if you don't understand it. Just sit with it for a little while.

If you have a particular problem or question, something you would like help with, ask for what you need. Again, just sit quietly, and notice anything that comes to you and stay with that. If it feels like nothing in particular comes to you right now, that's okay. Just let it go. Be open to it coming later, perhaps in some other form. Otherwise, just stay with whatever comes to you. Then you can just sit quietly and be. Take as long as you wish with this process.

When you feel complete for the moment, give thanks to your spiritual being. Ask for any support you need. If it feels right to you, make a commitment to come inside as often as you can to cultivate the relationship with your own spirit, to learn to listen to whatever your inner guidance may tell you.

Now become aware of your body once again, and notice how you are feeling right now. Notice if your body is feeling different than it did before you started this meditation. Without opening your eyes, become aware of your surroundings. Sense and feel what's around you. When you are ready, slowly begin to open your eyes.

As you open your eyes and come back into the outside world, see if you can still maintain that feeling of connection to your inner world. That connection to the inside is like the roots of the tree of our life. If we can remember that our roots go deep into our internal spiritual world, it can be the foundation for everything in our lives.

When you're ready, slowly stretch your body. Get up gently, and go about your life.

Sometimes when you do this meditation, you may feel that nothing happens. Or you may find at times that you obsess about certain thoughts or feelings and can't really relax. This is normal and natural. As you practice this meditation regularly for awhile, you will probably find it gets easier to drop into a relaxed, quiet state of mind. If not, then you might try listening to a meditation tape, taking a class in meditation or relaxation techniques, or trying a different kind of spiritual practice.

Some techniques people find helpful for learning to relax so they can meditate are: focusing on your breath (sitting with eyes closed and noticing your breath as it enters and leaves your nostrils); dancing to your favorite music until you sweat; sitting quietly while focusing on an object such as a flower, the flame of a candle, or a sound; chanting, drumming, or listening to calming and repetitive music.*

---

* Many simple and powerful meditations and spiritual practices can be found in the book *Coming Home: The Return to True Self* by Martia Nelson (see Recommended Resources).

CHAPTER 3

~

HEALING
THE
MENTAL LEVEL

The mental level of life encompasses our intellect, ideas, beliefs, and basic life philosophy. In order to clear and heal the mental level, we need to become conscious of our thought patterns and underlying belief systems. We need to educate ourselves about other ideas and eventually enable ourselves to consciously choose the beliefs, values, and philosophies that make most sense to us and support our conscious evolution.

We have all picked up certain beliefs and attitudes about the world through the early influences of our family, religion, schooling, culture, and life experiences. Many of these beliefs are quite unconscious; we are not at all aware that we hold them. It's as if we view the world through tinted glasses we don't even realize we're wearing. We believe the world is just that color. If we become aware of the glasses, we can choose to take them off and see the world quite differently. Similarly, once we become aware of our core beliefs, we can make more conscious choices about our ideas, attitudes, and expectations.

A wonderful story told by Deepak Chopra illustrates how our beliefs control our lives. When training baby elephants in India, trainers start by chaining one hind leg of the animal to a large tree. In a short time the elephant becomes so accustomed to the chain that he no longer tries to free himself. The trainer then reduces the size of the chain. In time, the elephant is so conditioned to the restraint that even a tiny string around the foot will stop him. Yet it is certainly not the cord that holds him; rather, it is his belief that he is restrained.

Like the elephant, our belief systems color our experience of the world, and we tend to keep interpreting and recreating our world based on our core beliefs about ourselves, other people, and life in general. However, as we mature and have new and different life experiences, new perspectives may challenge our beliefs. Every moment of our lives we are involved in an ongoing process of sorting out and evolving our philosophy, whether or not we are conscious of it.

To become aware of your core beliefs, pay attention to your thoughts, especially noticing the chronic, repetitive ones that run through your mind. If you can, begin to write down some of your repetitive thoughts and beliefs. This simple but profound step helps to bring them to consciousness. Talking to a therapist or a friend about them can help you begin to detach from old belief systems. Whenever you notice such a recurring thought pattern, think about where it came from. Did you pick it up from one of your parents, or someone else in your early life? Is there an underlying core belief in which these thoughts are rooted?

As you gain more awareness of your thought patterns and underlying belief systems, you may recognize that some of them support you in your personal growth and well-being, while others limit you or interfere with your process of creating satisfaction and fulfillment in your life.

As we become more conscious of our core beliefs, the ones that no longer serve us automatically begin to dissolve, and the ones that support us begin to take root. There is an exercise on identifying your inner rules at the end of this chapter that can help you with this process.

To experience balance, integration, and well-being in our lives, the mental level must support and harmonize with the other three levels of our existence. We need to have a spiritual philosophy that gives us a broader perspective and helps us find meaning in our lives. We need to have an understanding and acceptance of our own emotions that helps us to love ourselves. We need to know how to care for our physical bodies in a healthy way.

For example, if you believe your physical body is inferior to your spiritual self and that it is unworthy of your care or attention, you are holding onto a mental attitude that will cause conflict and lack of well-being in your system. But if you re-educate yourself to understand how important and worthy your physical body is, and you learn to take good care of it, your entire system will feel more balanced and harmonious.

In the process of becoming more conscious, we are constantly learning new ideas, viewpoints, and philosophies, and weighing them against the ones we already hold. Gradually, we begin letting go of the old ideas that are too limiting for us, while retaining the ones that still serve us and incorporating new ones that are more expansive, deepening, and empowering.

For example, I used to believe there wasn't much I could do about the circumstances of my life, that I didn't have much power to change them. Then I learned the idea that I create my own experience of reality.* I found that idea much more empowering, so I eventually chose to adopt that belief system. As I did this, I began to experience the world in a very different way and began to see that I really could have a great deal of power over my life's circumstances.

I grew up believing I would choose a life career and go to college for many years in order to achieve my goals. But after

---

* For an explanation and discussion of this concept, please see my book *The Path of Transformation*.

four years of college and a bachelor's degree, I still didn't know exactly what I wanted to do! In the process of searching I discovered a new philosophy: By trusting and following my intuitive guidance and creative impulses, my life would develop in interesting and fulfilling ways. A fascinating and successful career has unfolded from following this belief system — and as it turns out, I never went back to college.

~

Popular Misconceptions

Many people, especially people involved in the New Age, are confused about the process of healing the mental level. They think they must always practice positive thinking, using this technique to block out their so-called negative thoughts. They are afraid their negative thoughts will hurt them. Perhaps they have been stuck in negative thoughts and feelings at one time in their lives. Now that they are feeling more positive, they don't want to acknowledge any negativity for fear of slipping back into a gloomy perspective. So they deny or repress all their negative thoughts and concentrate only on the positive ones.

For some people this works fairly well for a while, but eventually all those denied, repressed thoughts and feelings come to the surface one way or another. Thoughts are energy patterns and they must go somewhere. They don't just disappear because you want them to. That's why many people who attempt to practice positive thinking are quite surprised to discover that efforts to get rid of their negative thinking actually make matters worse. Rather than diminishing their negative thoughts and feelings they find themselves caught up in them even more. This is a very predictable outcome of focusing only on the positive.

Remember that the first step in any healing process is always acknowledgment and acceptance of what is true right now. We don't heal anything by trying to block it out, get rid of it, or pretend it doesn't exist. We heal it by accepting that it's there, then becoming aware that there are other possible choices. So, we need to acknowledge and accept our so-called negative thoughts as part of who we are, while at the same time recognizing and developing other perspectives and ideas that give us more expansive possibilities. Again, this takes practice and should be viewed as a long term commitment.

Another common New Age fallacy is that you can change your whole life just by changing your thoughts. In fact, becoming aware of your thoughts and allowing them to change naturally is an important part of healing your life. But the mental level is only one of four aspects. Deep change can only occur when we work on and integrate all four levels.

Many people think thoughts and feelings are the same. They lump them together under the word "mind" — as in body, mind, and spirit. They believe that if you change your thoughts, you change your feelings, too. In reality, thoughts and feelings, although connected, are quite different. Just changing how you think about something doesn't immediately change your feelings. We will discuss this further in the next chapter, when we explore healing the emotional level.

Healing the Inner Critic

One big problem many of us experience on the mental level is an overactive "inner critic" — a voice inside that constantly tells you what you've done wrong, tells you how inadequate you are, compares you unfavorably with others, and so on. This problem actually has its roots in the emotional level, but plays out on the mental level through repetitive self-critical thoughts.

If you have a strong inner critic, it can make your life quite miserable by always making negative comments about everything that you do. This may prevent you from expressing yourself freely, exploring your creativity, trying new things, and taking necessary risks in life. Ultimately, the inner critic can cause you to feel unnecessarily discouraged and depressed.

Fortunately, it is possible to become conscious of your inner critic, work with it, and eventually transform it into an ally rather than an enemy. Drs. Hal and Sidra Stone have done wonderful work helping people heal their inner critics (as well as helping them become conscious of the many other inner voices or selves we all have within us.) Their book, *Embracing*

Your Inner Critic: Turning Self Criticism into a Creative Asset, and two audiotapes, *Meet Your Inner Critic* and *Meet Your Inner Critic II* are extremely helpful. (See Recommended Resources.)

~

Many Kinds of Intelligence

Some people have been wounded on the mental level by being told during their childhood that they were stupid, or by being compared unfavorably to a sibling or a classmate. Also, many girls receive the direct or indirect message that females are less intelligent than males, or that intelligence is unimportant or undesirable in women.

Another problem is that many people with more intuitive, right-brain learning styles don't do well in our left-brain, logically-oriented school systems. They may have mistakenly drawn the conclusion that they aren't very smart, when in reality they have a different type of intelligence.

People who have suffered these types of traumas in early life may have learned to doubt, discount, or deny their own intellect. In this case, the mental healing process must involve reclaiming one's own native intelligence and learning to trust it.

Our society tends to recognize and reward only one or two kinds of intelligence. Yet there are actually many different kinds of intelligence, and they are all useful and important.

In his book *Frames of Mind: The Theory of Multiple Intelligences*, Howard Gardner suggests that we each have at least seven distinctly different types of intelligence. Each of these seven intelligences operates from a different part of the brain and is relatively independent of the others, with its own timetable for development and growth.

Gardner identifies the seven intelligences as follows:

- *Logical-Mathematical Intelligence*: The ability to organize, quantify, and understand numerical symbols, abstractions, and logic.

- *Linguistic Intelligence*: The ability to understand and use language.

- *Spatial Intelligence*: The ability to perceive the physical world and to imagine how things fit together.

- *Bodily-Kinesthetic Intelligence:* The ability to use one's body in highly differentiated and skilled ways, for example, as a dancer, athlete, or mime.

- *Musical Intelligence*: The ability to recognize and reproduce musical tone, rhythm and pattern.

- *Intrapersonal Intelligence*: The ability to be in touch with one's own feelings and sense of self.

- *Interpersonal Intelligence*: The ability to notice other people's feelings and experiences, and to communicate with and influence other people.

Every individual is more developed in certain kinds of intelligence than in others. In each kind of intelligence is a clue to the gifts we have come here to give. Ironically, we are often the last to recognize and acknowledge our own talents and abilities. We tend to be somewhat blind to the things we do best. We live with our own genius every day and it just seems normal to us.

It can be interesting to ask a close friend what they think your greatest strengths and abilities are. It's also useful to try to identify other people's types of intelligence so you can get acquainted with the variety of ways that people are gifted.

There is an exercise at the end of this chapter that can help you recognize and develop your own unique abilities.

Interestingly enough, I have known a number of people who found that returning to school as an adult was a very healing experience. One friend of mine who had never graduated from high school studied for and completed his high school equivalency exam at the age of 37, then went to college and earned a bachelor's and then a master's degree in his chosen field. Needless to say, he was enormously empowered by this experience.

Many other friends and students of mine have returned to college to complete a degree or study a particular subject. These days, there are many excellent programs geared towards working adults, both in conventional colleges and alternative institutions. Being an adult, in touch with your passion and knowing what direction you want to follow, may afford you a very different experience in school than when you were younger, and the difference may transform your entire perspective on yourself and your life.

On the other hand, if you don't have a strong desire to pursue an education in this form, returning to school could simply be a miserable repeat of your earlier life experience. If you feel you need some kind of structure or support in your mental development but are not drawn to traditional schooling, look around for alternative possibilities. Ask your inner guidance for direction, and explore any options that sound interesting.

Exercise: Becoming Aware of Your Inner Rules

Our core belief systems often show up in our lives in the form of rules we consciously or unconsciously try to follow. Identifying these rules and working with them can help you have more choice about which ones are appropriate for you. Here are two exercises that help you get in touch with the inner rules that may be strongly influencing your life. The first is a written exercise and the second is a guided meditation. Read through the meditation completely before guiding yourself through this process.

For the written exercise you will need a notebook or several sheets of paper and a pen. Sit where you can write comfortably. At the top of each page write down one of the following topics, then leave the rest of the page blank:

- spiritual
- social/relationships
- work/school
- body

There should be four pages, with one of these topics at the top of each.

First, we'll examine the main rules or beliefs you learned as a child. Some of these may have been directly given to you by a parent, grandparent, teacher, or someone else important in your life. Many of these rules may have come indirectly or unconsciously from watching how others behave, through implication, or absorbing them from your culture. Remember not to give a value to the rules, such as good or bad. Just list as many as you can remember.

Think back to when you were a child. What kind of rules were you taught about being spiritual? For example, *"You should pray everyday,"* or *"Do unto others as you would have them do unto you."*

On the page marked spiritual, write down any rules

or strong beliefs you learned about spirituality as a child. Take as long as you want to do this. You may even add to this list over a period of several days.

On the second page, marked "social/relationships," list the rules you learned about appropriate social behavior. For example, *"Don't run or talk loudly in the house,"* or *"Children should be seen and not heard."* Also, what did you learn about the right way of being in relationships with others? For example, *"Always be considerate of other people's feelings,"* or *"Men are primarily responsible for earning a living; women are primarily responsible for raising children and keeping a home."*

Again, take as long as you need to do this. Don't hesitate to add to this list. You may even want to confer with a family member to jog your memory.

On the next page, marked "work/school," write down any rules you learned about the areas of work and school. For example, *"Work hard and get good grades,"* or *"The only way to get ahead in life is to have a good education,"* and so on.

On the page marked "body," write down any rules you learned about your appearance, food, health, hygiene, sports and play, and sexuality. There are a lot of sub-categories here, so take your time with this. You might have learned that famous admonition we all love so much: *"Always wear clean underwear in case you're in an accident."* Or you might have been told, *"Always clean your plate; think of the starving children in less advantaged countries."* Another typical rule for many women was to remain a virgin until you're married. Go through each subcategory in this body section and write down as many rules as you can think of that you learned as a child. Use as many sheets of paper as you need.

Now that you've completed this list, let's look at the rules you're *currently* living by. Some of these might be the same as the ones from childhood. Others might be totally different or even the opposite. Using the back side of each sheet of paper or another sheet, redo this exercise, going through the same categories. This time write down any rules you are in touch with that you consciously or unconsciously try to live by today. Take as much time as you need to do this. When you've written down all the rules you can think of, read through them and make a star by the ones that still really work for you. In other words, select the rules you still live by and that guide you positively.

When you have starred the rules that presently work for you, read through your lists again and

42

make an "x" by any rules that seem overly harsh, restrictive, dogmatic, difficult to live up to, or ones that you no longer believe.

Some of these rules may no longer be necessary and may not be in harmony with your true needs. In reviewing the rules marked by an "x," pick one from any of the categories that you'd like to change or let go. Write out a new belief you'd like to follow instead.

Let's say you have a belief that you must always complete all your work before you can relax or have fun, and that rule really drives you to work too hard and have very little enjoyment. One way to rewrite that rule is

"It's okay to relax and have fun and leave some work to be done later."

For each category — spiritual, social/relationships, work/school, body — pick two rules from the starred list that you want to live your life by and remind yourself to consciously embrace them. Also review the rules you put an "x" by and pick two from each category that you want to begin redefining or letting go of in your life. You may want to rewrite them in a similar fashion to the example above.

Exercise: New Beliefs Meditation

Here is a meditation to help you bring these new beliefs into your life. Please read through the entire meditation before closing your eyes and experiencing it.

Get in a comfortable position either sitting or lying down. If you are sitting, have your back straight and firmly supported and your feet on the floor. If you are lying down, lie on your back in a comfortable way, maybe with a pillow under your knees for lower back support. Before you close your eyes, think about one of the new rules or beliefs that you want to incorporate into your life.

Now close your eyes, take a deep breath, and as you exhale, relax your body. Take another deep breath, and as you exhale, relax your body a bit more. Keep taking a few deep breaths, and as you exhale each one, relax your body as deeply and completely as you can and let go of any tension you might be holding. Let your body become very relaxed.

Keep breathing deeply, and as you exhale each breath, relax your mind and let your thoughts go. As each new thought arises in your mind, let it go. Allow your mind to slow down.

Let your awareness move into a deep quiet place inside and just rest quietly in this space.

When you're ready, bring to your mind a new belief that you want to create for yourself. For example: *"When I trust and follow my intuition, my life unfolds exactly as it should."* Say it to yourself slowly, firmly, and clearly. Repeat this new belief to yourself several times. Each time really think about it, feel it, and affirm that you can have this new belief effortlessly incorporated into your life.

Now imagine yourself as you would feel and behave with this new belief. How would your life be different if you operated by this new belief instead of the old one? You might get a mental picture of this, or you might sense it or just think about it. Imagine this belief as if it was already true. It is not important whether or not you can clearly visualize anything about this new belief. Just the act of setting your intention is enough.

When you are ready, once again become aware of your body. Notice how your body is feeling right now. Notice what parts are very relaxed and what parts need to stretch because they have become somewhat stiff or sore. Before you open your eyes, get a sense of your surroundings, then slowly open your eyes and come back fully present in the room.

Once you are up and moving around, find a piece of paper and pen or use your journal to write down any thoughts, images, or feelings that occurred during your meditation. They may not make sense to you right now and this is perfectly fine. Don't evaluate these thoughts, feelings, or images — just note them. These notes may trigger ideas for you sometime in the near future when you reflect back on them.

I strongly suggest you revisit this meditation using a number of the new beliefs you formulated. It is best to do this meditation again over the next few days or weeks so these beliefs are fresh. Take each belief, guide yourself in this meditation, and note your thoughts, feeling, or images as they arise. Remember your nonrational mind is at work when you meditate, so don't feel that you must understand all of its messages immediately.

Exercise: Rediscovering Your Native Intelligence

Think about the various kinds of intelligences listed earlier in the chapter or any other kinds of intelligence you may have observed on your own. What kinds of intelligence do you have? You may actually have a unique combination of several of the intelligences noted earlier, plus one or more others that you may have thought of yourself.

To help you open your eyes to your own intelligence, remember back to the activities you gravitated toward as a child. Did you enjoy:

- Exploring nature?
- Reading?
- Making up stories?
- Playing with animals?
- Putting on plays?
- Taking things apart to see how they work?
- Sports?
- Music?
- Other interests? What were they?

Take a moment to write down a list of things you do well or you really like to do. You may also include things you loved to do as a child that you no longer have time for or have somehow lost contact with. Is there a common thread running through them? Follow this thread. It will lead you to your own unique intelligence.

As you get in touch with your own intelligence, you may also recognize that you were rewarded, discouraged, belittled, or encouraged in the area of your greatest interest. If you had negative experiences where your native intelligence is concerned, start reaffirming your abilities right now by recognizing that your natural gifts and unique intelligence are found in those activities and interests. There is a reason you gravitated in that direction during your early years. The inner compass that pointed you in that particular direction is rarely, if ever, wrong.

If you need to do some healing around your gifts, look for ways you might start to develop those early interests. Pursue skills and knowledge in that area through classes, or by getting to know other people who have successful careers in your field of interest, reading more about it, and — perhaps most important of all — doing it for yourself, starting right now.

Begin following your heart with the faith that your early interests are trustworthy indicators, revealing your true gifts. Find a way to get hands-on experience: If your early interest was writing, start a writing journal, take a writing class, or read a book on the kind of writing you'd like to do whether it be screenplays, novels, or essays. If you are interested in mechanical things, find a broken-down machine that intrigues you and take it apart. If working with people is your passion, sign up to volunteer at an agency that helps people, maybe in an age group that intrigues you, such as children or seniors. Such firsthand involvement not only revives and reaffirms your interests and your "native intelligence," it also gets you on your way to actualizing these most important parts of your self that may have been lost.

CHAPTER 4

~

HEALING
THE
EMOTIONAL LEVEL

Many of us find working on the spiritual level pleasant and inspiring, and most of us are relatively comfortable exploring the mental realm because we live in such a mentally-oriented society.

However, a lot of us get stuck at the level on which emotional healing needs to take place. Most of us are frightened and uncomfortable about the prospect of doing deep emotional healing work. We are afraid of dredging up old pain and perhaps being overwhelmed by it. We wonder what the point is in focusing on unresolved emotional issues and uncomfortable feelings. We don't realize that effective emotional healing will actually free us from dragging that pain around for the rest of our lives.

We live in a culture that has amazingly little understanding of emotion and doesn't really value the realm of feeling. In fact, most of us are taught, subtly or overtly, to fear our emotions — that feelings are unpredictable, irrational, dangerous, and we should try to keep them firmly under control. We have learned, to one degree or another, to hide and deny our feelings — even from ourselves. We've learned to bury most of our feelings deep inside and show the world only what seems safe, which usually isn't very much of our emotional nature.

In childhood we may have gotten a lot of messages, like *"There's no reason to feel that way,"* or *"Don't get so excited,"* or the classic *"Big boys (or girls) don't cry."* Recently an adult friend of mine was telling me of his father's death and his mother's admonition to him not to cry at his father's funeral, because it would look like a sign of weakness! The attitudes we were taught root very deeply in our psyche. In this story you can see the heritage of repressed feelings my friend's mother was taught and passed on to her son.

Generally, we are taught not to feel any emotion too strongly — even love or joy — because we want to stay cool and in control. We're especially taught not to feel or acknowledge so-called negative emotions, such as fear, sadness, hurt, anger, or despair.

While most of us have learned to repress our feelings, some of us have the opposite problem: We are too easily overwhelmed by our emotions and have difficulty maintaining any emotional equilibrium. We are often carrying the repressed emotions of other people around us, experiencing and expressing everyone else's feelings, as well as our own. Still others are stuck in one particular emotion and are constantly reacting from that place — anger perhaps, or fear. These are all symptoms of emotional imbalances that need healing.

Unfortunately, many traditional spiritual philosophies and New Age belief systems reinforce the tendency to repress certain emotions by encouraging us to rise above them, or try to focus on more acceptable feelings, such as unconditional love. I've heard many spiritually inclined teachers advise people to let go of anger and other so-called negative feelings. Unfortunately, they usually don't explain exactly how one is supposed to do this letting go, leaving the students floundering and wondering why they can't seem to magically make all their negative feelings disappear. If a method is recommended, it is usually something like this: Just put that feeling aside and focus on a positive experience or feeling. Or the student is encouraged to identify with and develop only the spiritual aspect of his or her being, seen as the true self, and to view the personality with all its emotions and feelings as the false self, or the ego to be overcome.

These approaches are just good, old-fashioned denial dressed up in an appealing costume. Emotional denial is dangerous and destructive to the human psyche, because we are attempting to reject and eliminate an integral and important part of ourselves. Ultimately, it can never work. How can we get rid of a core part of who we are? It also causes us to be in intense conflict with ourselves — the part of us that thinks we shouldn't have the feelings fighting the part of us that actually has these feelings. The truth is, we cannot deny, control, or attempt to change our feelings this way without eventually causing more emotional damage to ourselves.

All Our Emotions Are Important

Our feelings are a deep, important part of our lives and they need to be respected and honored. None of our emotions are intrinsically bad or negative. We call things negative because we don't understand them, and so we fear them.

Emotions are a significant aspect of our human experience, and they all exist for a reason. Rather than rejecting or avoiding them, we need to discover the gift each one brings us. They are messages to us, letting us know something we need to pay attention to.

If you are sad, that feeling may be revealing that you need something. If you honor the feeling and ask what it is about, it can guide you to awareness of your need. Sadness may be letting you know that it's time to allow yourself to grieve as you let go of something or someone. Tears are the river of life washing away the old to make way for something new. An ancient proverb says, *"For every tear shed, a day is added to your life."*

Anger can be our protection when we feel hurt or frightened. Anger can also be a way we begin to reclaim our power if we have disowned it or given it away to others. If properly handled, it can help us learn to stand up for ourselves, speak our truth, and set our boundaries.

Of course, we all know that anger can sometimes be hurtful and destructive, which is why many of us are so afraid of it. However, anger usually comes out in a harmful way for one of two reasons: 1) It has been held in and repressed for so long that it finally (or periodically) bursts out in an explosive, violent way. 2) It is habitually used by someone to cover and conceal their deeper, more vulnerable feelings such as fear, sadness, or hurt. Fortunately, it is possible to heal these patterns and learn to express anger in clean, clear, appropriate, and nonharmful ways.

Fear is an emotion that many people strive to get rid of or at least hide. Yet fear has an important function — it warns us that something may be dangerous or difficult, so that we pay attention, evaluate the situation, and choose the appropriate action. If we completely eliminated fear, we would do many dangerous and, most likely, fatal things. Of course, some people are overwhelmed or controlled by fear; the solution is not to eliminate fear entirely, but to bring it into proper balance.

A popular concept in the New Age is that fear is the opposite of love, so if we want to experience love, we must let go of fear. I would say instead that we need to love our fear, that is, learn to accept our fear as a valid aspect of our being. When we can truly accept ourselves with all our emotions and feelings, we experience real unconditional love for ourselves, which allows us to feel compassion and love for others. When we are not battling ourselves internally, trying to overcome certain emotions, we can develop an attitude of peaceful self-acceptance, which allows us to open to our spiritual essence and integrate it into our human existence.

Life is made up of paradoxes. In order to completely feel anything, we must be able to experience the fullness of its opposite. To feel real strength, we must accept our weaknesses. To feel truly powerful, we must allow ourselves to acknowledge our vulnerability. To feel profound joy, we must embrace our sadness. Kahlil Gibran has a wonderful line in his book, *The Prophet*, that says, "*The deeper that sadness carves into your being, the more joy you can contain.*"

Our emotions are like the weather, constantly changing, and as with the weather, it's fruitless to try to control your feelings. Instead, we can learn to appreciate all our different moods and emotions. Just as we can enjoy a sunny day and a stormy day in different ways, we can learn to find the beauty in joy and in sadness.

Our emotions are what we feel as the life force moves through us. When we don't experience our feelings fully and allow them to move through us in a natural way, the life energy in those feelings becomes lodged in our bodies. This causes many problems on all the levels — emotional, mental, spiritual, and physical. In my experience working with thousands of people, I have found that blocked emotions are a primary cause, or a contributing factor, in many or most physical ailments. So emotional healing can be an important part of physical healing.

Accepting our emotions allows us to feel them. Learning to communicate them constructively and appropriately allows them to move through us easily and naturally. This enables the full free flow of the life force through our physical bodies, bringing emotional and physical healing.

Repressing feelings = blocked energy = emotional and physical ailments

Experiencing feelings = free flowing energy = emotional and physical health and well-being

~

The Difference Between Thoughts and Feelings

One of the first steps in healing the emotional level is learning the difference between what we think and what we feel. Often when we are asked, *"How do you feel about this?"* we say something like, *"I think it's a good idea."*

How you feel about something and what you think about it

may be quite different. You might believe on a rational level that something makes sense, yet you may feel unhappy about it.

Let's say someone offers you a business opportunity. In your mind it might seem like a great idea, yet you might feel emotionally uncomfortable about it. Perhaps you feel intimidated by the person involved, or the change would mean a lot of emotional upheaval that you're not sure you want. It's important to acknowledge and honor both levels of truth — the mental and the emotional. Allow yourself to be with this paradox for a while. Ask your inner intuitive guidance to show you your next step. Usually, clarity will begin to emerge from this process.

As I mentioned before, many spiritual teachers confuse the mental and the emotional levels, or treat them as one, lumping them together under the term "mind". However, they are very different. We are feeling beings long before we develop our rational minds. Our thoughts are much more connected to our conscious mind and will, whereas our feelings come from a deeper, less rational place.

To some degree we can consciously choose our thoughts, but the only choice we have about our feelings is how we handle them. We can choose to deny our feelings, indulge them and act them out, or consciously acknowledge and work with them. If you are upset with somebody you can pretend everything is okay, which is denial. Or you can yell at them and perhaps hit them or throw things, which would be indulgent acting out. Or you can acknowledge to yourself, and if appropriate, to the other person, that you are feeling angry and hurt, and take time to really acknowledge the feelings. Interestingly enough, when you fully allow yourself your own feelings you usually don't have as much need to vent them on someone else.

If a feeling truly is overwhelmingly strong, you may need to talk about it with a supportive friend or a therapist before you know what, if any, action needs to take place.

~

Doing Your Emotional Healing Work

The essence of emotional healing is this: being in touch with what you are feeling, being able to say honestly what you are feeling to at least one other human being, and having that person respond with empathy, as in, "Oh, I understand." This lets us know that we're not bad, wrong, or crazy for feeling what we feel and that we're not alone in our experience.

When we were infants and children we had many strong feelings. What we needed was to have people acknowledge and respond to these feelings in appropriate ways. For example, we needed to hear things like, "I understand that you're very upset," or "I can see that you're feeling really sad." In essence, as children we needed reflection and validation of our feelings from our parents, families, teachers, and the surrounding world. We needed assurance that we have a right to our feelings, that they aren't wrong or bad. We needed to feel that others can understand and empathize with us when we experience strong feelings. We needed to be allowed to have our own feeling experience. No matter how hard parents try — and they all do the best that they can — children inevitably experience some degree of emotional hurt, neglect, and abandonment. Because we're so vulnerable as children, we are deeply wounded by these experiences and carry them inside us for the rest of our lives, or until we do our conscious emotional healing work.

In emotional healing work we learn to give ourselves, and allow ourselves to receive from others, what we didn't receive as young children. We learn to accept and experience all our feelings, and when appropriate, to communicate these feelings in a way that allows others to understand us. We open the way to our emotional healing through the experience of having at least one other person hear, understand, and empathize with us.

If we have denied or stuffed down a lot of our feelings, we may need to have a safe place and an experienced guide (a professional counselor or therapist) to help us begin to get in touch with, experience, and release our emotions. Then we need to develop tools for staying current with our feelings, by allowing ourselves to acknowledge and experience them as they arise.

It's important to get in touch with the needs underneath our feelings, and to learn how to communicate those needs effectively. Underneath most of our emotions are our basic needs for love, acceptance, security, and self-esteem. We need to get to know the vulnerable child who still lives deep inside each of us, and to learn to become the loving parent our own inner child requires. If we want to experience the full range of our being in this lifetime, we need to commit ourselves to heal the emotional wounds from our childhood and early life.

Sometimes people fear that exploring the emotional wounds from childhood means blaming their parents or others, which they do not wish to do. It is true that in the process of deep emotional healing it is often important to acknowledge to ourselves any old, buried feelings of hurt, resentment, and sometimes blame of ourselves or others. The magical thing is that once those feelings are consciously acknowledged and experienced in a safe, supportive environment, they generally dissolve, or shift into feelings of acceptance, compassion, and forgiveness.

Often, people try to jump directly to forgiveness, not wishing to experience the more uncomfortable emotions. While this is sometimes effective, in many cases it is a kind of forced forgiveness, laid over the still unresolved emotions which often resurface later. Once the other feelings are acknowledged and worked through, forgiveness takes place naturally and automatically.

At some point in the emotional healing process, it may or may not be necessary to communicate with the actual people involved. This is a very individual matter and every situation is different. The person or people (parents, other family

61

members, ex-spouses or whoever) may no longer be alive, or may be completely unreceptive or unable to hear any of your feelings. In that case, writing a long, honest letter that you never send, or bringing that person to mind in meditation and imagining that you communicate everything you need to say, can be effective ways of completing a healing process. Oftentimes, once you've worked through a deep part of your own emotional healing process, things shift dramatically in your long-term relationships without anything needing to be said in words. Or you may find that at some point you need to sit down and have a heart-to-heart talk with someone in order to clear the past.

Profound emotional healing takes time. It cannot be rushed or forced. It needs to unfold in its own time, sometimes taking a number of years to move through the deeper levels. Fortunately, as each layer is healed, life becomes more and more fulfilling and rewarding, and does actually lighten up.

～

Getting Support

In order to work through deep emotional healing, most of us need help and support. For some of us that support may be in the form of loving friends and family, but at times we may need more skilled and objective help, in the form of a therapist or a support group.

Many people feel afraid or ashamed to seek assistance from

a professional counselor or therapist, and it's no wonder. Hollywood movies invariably portray therapists as ineffective idiots or scheming manipulators. Our cultural conditioning tells us that we should be self-sufficient and in control, that it's shameful and embarrassing to need help. Some of us may feel that we are smart enough to figure it out for ourselves. As I stressed before, you cannot think your way out of your emotional wounding. As human beings, we do need support at times. It's a mark of strength and courage to know when you need assistance and to reach out to appropriate people. I've been in therapy many times in my life when I needed special help working through deep issues. It has always been immensely beneficial to me.

The trick is to find a good psychotherapist who really knows how to help you through this process. It is sometimes rather shocking to me to discover how few therapists understand how to do deep emotional healing. Many therapists function more on a mental level, helping their clients understand themselves and gain insights about their psychological functioning, which can be quite valuable at the appropriate time. However, they may not know how to guide their clients through the process of experiencing their deeper feelings. In order to facilitate others successfully, we need to have done our own deep healing work, and many therapists have done little of this. They may, in fact, be uncomfortable with strong emotions and unconsciously steer their clients away from expressing them. Many people have come to my workshops after years of therapy and been shocked to discover a whole level of feeling they had never touched before.

Fortunately, all this is slowly changing. More and more therapists are going through their own emotional healing and learning how to effectively guide others through theirs.

There are many different kinds of therapists and counselors, with a wide range of effectiveness. What's right for one person will not necessarily work for another. So don't be afraid to shop around. Ask friends for recommendations. Set up an initial interview, or try a few sessions to see if you feel comfortable with the therapist and if their way of working is helpful to you.

A good therapist helps you get in touch with your feelings and supports you in learning to trust yourself. Good therapy empowers you to express yourself honestly and authentically, and to be who you really are. Generally, you begin to feel some significant movement in yourself and your life as a result of therapy within the first few weeks or months.

Emotional healing is an ongoing process. We move through it layer by layer, sometimes gently, sometimes intensely. Everyone is different, and we each have our own rhythm and timing.

Here's the good news: Emotional healing really does work! It is possible, in time, to heal the old emotional wounds so that they are no longer painful feelings we try to run away from or stuff down inside of us. Instead, our painful past experiences can ripen into deep wisdom. In the process, we can learn to become comfortable with all our emotions and bring them into a natural, healthy balance.

Exercise: Emotional Energy Scan

Here is a meditation that can help you stay in touch with your emotions. This is an especially good one to do when you first wake up or in the evening, before you go to sleep. You can also use it anytime you start feeling emotionally uncomfortable or disconnected, or just need to check in with yourself on a feeling level.

Before you start this meditation, put your journal or a piece of paper and pen next to you.

Find a comfortable position for yourself either sitting up straight with your feet on the floor, or lying down on your back with a pillow under your knees for support.

Close your eyes and begin breathing deeply and slowly. Take a few deep breaths, and as you exhale each one, relax your body as deeply and completely as you can. Take another deep breath, and as you exhale, relax your mind and let your thoughts float away. Take as many breaths as you need to feel deeply relaxed. As each new thought comes up in your mind, let it float away and let your mind gradually slow down, becoming quiet and peaceful.

Allow your awareness to scan through your body, starting with your feet and working slowly up to your head. Notice the quality of energy your body is holding. Is your energy active and vibrating, or smooth and peaceful? Is it slow and sluggish, is it stuck anywhere? How do you experience this? Is there a mental image, thought, or feeling that tells you? Or is it just some inner sense?

Begin to tune in to how you're feeling emotionally right now, without trying to change anything. Become aware of how the energy feels in your body and how you feel emotionally. See if there is one place in your body where your energy and emotions feel linked. Notice if there's a specific physical sensation anywhere in your body: a tightness in your stomach, an ache in your heart, tension in your neck, shoulders, or head. If so, let your attention gently rest there and be with that part of you, in a caring, soothing way. Let yourself feel the quality of the sensations in that area of your body. Ask if there are any emotions related to this physical feeling. If this feeling could talk, what would it say to you?

Take your time — stay with this for a while. Be receptive to anything that comes up. Ask if there's anything you need right now, anything you need to be aware of, to do for yourself in this moment, or in your life. Again, be receptive to whatever comes to you — a thought, image, or feeling — in answer to this question.

Remind yourself that whatever you're feeling is okay. All our feelings are okay. Don't allow yourself to evaluate the answers, just receive them.

When you feel complete with this meditation, bring your awareness back to your whole body and notice how it's feeling now. Without opening your eyes, become aware of your surroundings. When you're ready, slowly open your eyes, stretch your body a little bit, and breathe deeply.

If you feel like it, this would be a good time to write in your journal. Note anything you experienced from the meditation and let yourself be specific about any dialogue you had with any part of your body, or any feeling. Also note what came to you in answer to the question, "What do I need right now in this moment of my life?"

Questions you may want to answer in your journal regarding this meditation are:

- What is the overall quality of energy in my body today?

- How did I receive signals about my physical and emotional energy?

- The specific area of my body that I noticed was _____. It was feeling _____. Its message to me was _____.

- The emotional feelings I got in touch with are _____.

- Can I accept and allow myself to be with these feelings?

- Any other insights I received during this meditation are _____.

CHAPTER 5

~

HEALING
THE
PHYSICAL LEVEL

Our overall well-being depends on our ability to take care of ourselves in the physical world. Specifically, this means keeping our physical bodies fit, healthy, and satisfied. More generally, it means functioning in the world in a way that allows us not only to survive but to thrive — being able to make a living and provide for our physical needs and desires. On a subtler level, it involves a certain awakeness to physical matters, being aware of what is going on in our bodies and our surroundings. Last, but certainly not least, it involves a healthy and balanced relationship with our planet and the natural world.

Until very recently, most of us hadn't received much information or encouragement or had many good role models for creating a healthy way of life. In fact, our cultural lifestyle has become increasingly sedentary and unnatural. More and more people live in cities without much access to nature, drive everywhere in automobiles rather than walking, work in air-conditioned buildings with no natural light or air, and eat unhealthy, over-processed foods. Even worse, we live such busy, stressful lives that we constantly push our bodies past their natural energy level, frequently using caffeine to keep us going at an artificial pace.

Because modern civilization places such emphasis on intellectual and technological development, we have become largely disconnected from the feelings and needs of our physical selves. Our attitude toward nature and our own bodies has been one of conquering and controlling rather than respecting, honoring, and cooperating.

Another contributing factor has been an attitude toward the body fostered by the traditional, transcendent, spiritual approach of most of our current world religions. The body in most religions is seen as the enemy of the spirit, the seat of our human needs, emotions, passions, and attachments. The goal of these spiritual philosophies is to subdue and rise above these human aspects. The body is seen as lowly, inferior to mind and spirit, or even downright evil. Thus, the physical body is ignored or denigrated.

To make matters worse, our scientific tradition has taught

us to focus on the external causes and cures of disease, and to ignore the subtler and more internal causes and healing processes. We see ourselves as victims of diseases that can simply descend on us at anytime, for no particular reason. This leaves us feeling helpless, with little power or responsibility for our own health. For this reason, we have become overly dependent on outside authorities, often handing over our entire decision-making power to medical professionals.

This emphasis on external cures has also caused us to become an amazingly drug-oriented culture. Sometimes it seems we're each searching for the magic pill or potion that can take away our pain and make us feel good, at least momentarily. We are all well aware of the epidemic of drug, alcohol, tobacco, caffeine, food, and other addictions we currently suffer, as we frantically try to cope with our emotional and spiritual pain by shutting it out. In the process, we shut out the signals of our physical bodies as well.

The truth is, we are born with a natural awareness of our bodies' needs and feelings, but we've learned to tune the body out, either ignoring it or controlling it with our mental ideas about what's good for it. We've lost touch with our sensitivity to what is going on inside us and around us. Many of us are scarcely aware of our bodies at all, unless they are in extreme physical distress; the body has to get sick in order to get our attention.

Fortunately, all this is beginning to change. There is a dawning awareness in our culture of the importance of such things as proper nutrition and regular exercise; many people are beginning to take more responsibility for creating and maintaining their own physical health and well-being.

Physical healing takes place as we learn to tune into, feel, and listen to our bodies. Our bodies usually know what they need. They communicate to us clearly and specifically, if we are willing to listen to them. We need to cultivate the art of understanding and interpreting their signals. The body is constantly communicating its need for the right food at the right time, for rest when it's weary, for movement, and for touch.

In order to accurately receive the body's messages, we have to first heal our own addictive processes — the false cravings we may have developed for certain substances or foods that block us from feeling what our bodies really need. Our bodies naturally crave what is good for them.

~

Dealing with Addictions

If you have substance or food addictions, the first step in your healing process is to seek help from a qualified counselor, support group, treatment program, or twelve-step program such as Alcoholics Anonymous, Narcotics Anonymous, or Overeaters Anonymous. The first impulse of everyone dealing with an addiction is to think we can handle it on our own, using our own will power, and that we don't need any outside help. Unfortunately, this thought process is all part of the classic pattern of addiction and simply becomes part of the vicious circle. Most people find that to really heal an addictive pattern, they need help and support from others who have experience with the problem.

There are always many good reasons and excuses not to get help: You don't have the time or money, you don't feel comfortable with the counselor or other people at the meeting, your problem isn't really that serious, and so on. Just keep in mind that if you do have an active addictive pattern, your life is essentially stuck, and you will be unable to progress very much in your healing process on any level until you get the appropriate help and support. Taking that step can be the greatest gift you ever give yourself (and to your loved ones as well!).

Once you do commit yourself to your recovery process, give yourself plenty of time, patience, and compassion. It took years to develop our old habits and ways of coping; it's also a long-term process to develop healthier ways of living. Once we can stop automatically responding in an addictive way for a while, we can begin to get in touch with our real physical, emotional, mental, and spiritual needs, and allow them to guide us.

~

Listening to the Body

Many people have an unconscious assumption that their body is their enemy. Imagine how bad the body must feel to be regarded this way, and how much inner conflict this attitude creates. It leads to an adversarial relationship in which we are constantly trying to control our bodies and whip them into shape.

Many of us need to stop trying so hard to control our bodies out of anxiety about our physical appearance, or even out of a sincere desire to be healthy and fit. We adopt a lot of rules about what is good for us and try to force our bodies to conform to them. Some of these ideas and rules may be positive in themselves, but if we apply them too rigidly they may cause problems — for example, trying to eat only nonfat foods. We may become too controlling about our diet or push ourselves too hard when we exercise. Then we are likely to rebel against our self-imposed rules by going to the opposite extreme. Of course, there is an important place for healthy discipline when it's not overdone.

We need to make friends with our bodies and learn to acknowledge and appreciate how they serve us. Think about the fact that they work 24 hours a day to keep us alive and as healthy as possible. Practice giving your body appreciation. Notice how much pleasure you derive from your physical senses: tasting food, watching a sunset, smelling the flowers, listening to music, receiving a massage.

The most effective approach I've found to healing the physical level is to learn to listen to the body's innate wisdom and do your best to follow it. Think of how animals in their natural habitat eat when they are hungry, rest when they are tired, and are generally filled with energy and vitality. Of course, our lives are complex. It is often difficult to pay attention to simple things, and seldom possible to be truly spontaneous. However, we can begin to cultivate the habit of checking in with our bodies on a regular basis to find out what they need.

Here are some of the basic needs of the body:

- Plenty of pure, fresh water.

- A simple, natural, well-balanced diet of wholesome and tasty foods.

- Plenty of rest, including a good night's sleep and a rest or nap during the day if needed.

- Fresh air and time outdoors each day.

- Regular movement and exercise that is enjoyable and appropriate to your capabilities.

- Physical touch, affection, and closeness.

- Sensual and sexual pleasure and expression.

As you learn to tune into your body, it will guide you in discovering when and how to fulfill these needs.

Our physical body is where all the other levels — the spiritual, mental, and emotional aspects of our being — reside in this life. Our bodies mirror and express our state of wellbeing or lack thereof on all the levels. A block or imbalance on the spiritual, mental, or emotional level eventually shows up in the physical body. So not only is the body constantly communicating its own needs, it is frequently trying to communicate the needs of the other three levels as well.

If we have unmet needs on any level we are unconscious of or ignoring, eventually our bodies try to let us know about it. For example, if you are pushing yourself to work so hard that your spiritual and emotional needs are going unmet, your body may get sick as a way of forcing you to slow down and go inside.

My belief is that almost all physical illnesses or accidents have spiritual, mental, or emotional elements, or a combination of all three. I find that this is especially true of emotional needs, since they are often the most repressed. Physical healing can be enhanced and sped up by dealing with the other levels *in addition to* the physical. So an illness, ailment, or accident is an indication that we need to look deeply at ourselves and our lives, and be willing to make changes when called for on any or all levels. Generally, it's a message that we need to look a little more deeply at our needs and feelings, take better care of ourselves, or be more true to ourselves in some way. It may be the symptom of an inner conflict we need to deal with more directly.*

Often the body speaks amazingly clearly and metaphorically. For example, the woman whose back aches because she's

---

*For more information about how the other levels can affect the physical, and many excellent exercises to help with healing all levels, I recommend the book, *Passion to Heal* by Echo Bodine. See Recommended Resources.

carrying too much responsibility, or the man who has a heart attack because he's pushing so hard that he's ignoring the needs of his own heart. Understanding what your body's trying to tell you may not always be easy. It requires time to cultivate your ability to listen, and can be helped by quiet contemplation, journal writing, or therapy.

Don't worry if you don't understand with your mind what your body is trying to communicate. If you are open, you may be getting the message on a different level. Don't accept anyone else's interpretation of what an illness means *unless it feels right to you!* At the end of this chapter, there is a meditation that may help you receive your body's wisdom by looking at the possible spiritual, mental, or emotional causes of an illness.

Beware of falling into a trap that happens to a lot of people in New Age circles, which is feeling guilty or blaming yourself for having an illness. The thinking goes like this, "If I had really done my inner work I wouldn't have created this illness, therefore, I must be an unconscious person and a failure."

Some teachers and healers contribute to this by assuring people that if they think the right thoughts, say the right affirmations, eat the right diet, or whatever, they should be in perfect health. In reality it's not so simple.

It's possible to eat a pure diet, meditate every day, exercise regularly, express your feelings often, use affirmations and visualization, and still get sick! The journey of life is complex and often mysterious. We can't always know exactly why something is happening. Remember that our soul uses every avenue available to educate and enlighten us.

Illness is not necessarily a negative occurrence even though it may feel that way. Like everything else that happens to us, it is an opportunity to learn and grow and deepen our experience and wisdom. As difficult as it can be to accept, any ailment can be viewed as a gift, an opportunity to look at ourselves and our lives and learn something. It presents a possibility for real change.

An ailment may serve a vitally important function for us. Many people who drive themselves hard don't learn how to slow down until an illness forces them to. That illness may save their life or vastly improve the quality of their life.

A friend of mine has been struggling for the past couple of years to change her lifestyle, to make more time to take care of her own needs, rather than focusing on the needs of others. She had a rude awakening this year when she came down with pneumonia. This forced her to stop all her activities and honor herself in a nurturing way she has always needed. She is now working on integrating rest and self-nurturing into her less busy life.

The most constructive and effective way to deal with an ailment is to acknowledge you have it and, are not guilty for having it, but wish to use the experience to deepen and expand your consciousness.

Naturally, it doesn't usually feel like an opportunity for change and growth at the time. Most likely, it feels painful, frightening, confusing, discouraging. Part of the healing process is to allow ourselves to experience those feelings. It can be helpful to put a kind of framework around the experience, one that goes something like this: "Even though this feels terrible and I don't understand it, I know that there is a gift of learning and healing for me here. I'm open to receiving that and understanding it at the appropriate time." This empowers our inner guidance to show us what we need to learn from the experience.

Don't assume that every illness is meant to be healed and that you have failed if you haven't managed to heal yourself. Some illnesses stay with us as teachers and reminders. For example, a friend of mine gets heart arrhythmia every time he overextends himself or takes on too much responsibility for others. This condition has forced him to become extremely conscious of his own needs and of taking care of himself properly.

~

Life-Threatening Illness

Obviously, with a life-threatening illness or accident, the growth process is greatly intensified. Many people find that a critical illness causes them to confront major issues and, through this confrontation, gain life-changing awareness.

Some illnesses are here to help someone transition into another plane of existence. Again, we need to be careful about judging ourselves or others for having a serious illness or for any of the results that follow. We need to understand that death can be a legitimate and positive choice, not a failure to heal. Who are we to judge the journey of our own or another person's soul?

My sense is that our physical death is a choice we make on some level consciously or unconsciously. At this stage of our evolution, most of us make this decision unconsciously, for example, we fall victim to an illness or fatal accident. Fortunately, we are becoming more aware of the process of death and dying, and learning something about how to honor and support that process. I believe that more and more of us will be able to choose to depart from our physical bodies when the right time comes, in a clear and conscious way.

My personal experience in working with people on deep levels indicates that when someone has a life-threatening illness, there is a part of that person that wants to die. Usually, they are completely or mostly unconscious of that part. Generally, they are only aware of the part of them that wants to live. If they can get in touch with the part that wants to die and bring it to conscious awareness, it's often possible to find out why that choice is being made.

By getting in touch with the parts that want to die and the parts that don't, it is possible to make the choice a more conscious one. Oftentimes, on a deep level, the person may be feeling that his or her emotional needs are not being met and has given up on life. By consciously discovering this, there is a possibility for a great deal of healing, which may result in an extended life or a more peaceful death. On a spiritual level, the person may feel that they have accomplished what they needed in this life, or that they can accomplish the next step more effectively on a different plane of existence, or in another physical lifetime.

Not long ago, a woman I'll call Carmen came to one of my week-long intensives. She had been diagnosed with an inoperable and incurable tumor and was in considerable grief and emotional pain. Through working with the part of her that wanted to live and the part of her (previously totally unconscious) that wanted to die, she came to a place of much greater understanding and acceptance of her own process. In the next few months, she did a tremendous amount of emotional healing, and completion with many important people in her life. One of the most touching scenes she described was being held on her mother's lap and rocked (she had never before felt truly nurtured by her mother). Not long after that she died very peacefully, with loving friends and family around her.

Another woman I know was diagnosed HIV positive a number of years ago. Since that time she has done a great deal of healing work on all levels, including working with the part of her that unconsciously wanted to die. Today she is extremely healthy and active, and in the last year married and gave birth to a beautiful, healthy girl.

I know the idea that we may have a part of us which unconsciously wants to die may be shocking or difficult to accept.

However, like anything else we become conscious of within ourselves, it can be a very healing awareness. If you wish to explore this idea, I suggest working with a counselor or therapist who has experience working with life-threatening illness, or a therapist trained in the technique of Voice Dialogue, explained in the following chapter.

~

Steps Toward Healing

Here are the three basic steps for healing your body:

- If you have an acute ailment, especially a serious one, the first step is to get the most immediate and effective treatment you can find.

- Once you have done this, or if you don't have any acute physical ailments to begin with, the next step is to develop ongoing ways to strengthen and maintain your physical health and well-being.

- The third step is to look into the emotional, mental, and spiritual factors that may be contributing to any physical problems, then get whatever help or support you need in healing those areas.

In terms of the first two steps, choosing a treatment method for a physical problem can be confusing. In this day and age we have many choices available, including: western allopathic medicine and surgery, classic Chinese medicine, ayurvedic medicine, homeopathy, herbology, naturopathy, acupuncture, chiropractic, massage and body work, exercise therapy, as well as diet and nutrition.

My personal feeling is that all these modalities, and others I may have failed to mention, do have value and are appropriate in particular situations. I've benefited from nearly all of them at certain times in my life. Many of them are part of my regular health-maintenance regime.

These days, there are an increasing number of holistically-oriented doctors who work with both mainstream medicine and alternative methods. These people can be invaluable in helping you sort out the appropriate treatment modalities. Two excellent resources are Dr. Andrew Weil, author of several books, including *Spontaneous Healing*, and Dr. Christiane Northrup, author of *Women's Bodies, Women's Wisdom*. In addition to their books, both these physicians have regular newsletters filled with interesting and relevant health information. (See Recommended Resources.)

It's important to find out what works for you, whether it's for maintaining your health, treating problems when they arise, or restoring strength and health following radical treatments, such as surgery. Oftentimes, the most effective treatment is one you trust and believe can help you. In my experience, the more acute the problem, the more likely it is that western medicine is called for, since it generally employs the strongest and fastest methods for dealing with immediate symptoms or the disturbance of normal physical function. For other problems or for ongoing care, some of the so-called alternative methods may be more effective. In many cases the skill, wisdom, and sensitivity of the practitioner may be a more important factor than the method they use.

Try not to give all your power and authority to any doctor or professional health practitioner. At times we need to trust their expertise and follow their advice but, if possible, we need to also balance our reliance on others with self-awareness and self-trust. We need to see our helping professionals not as the ultimate authority, but as guides assisting us along our path of healing.

Explore, discover, and learn as much as you can about the alternatives available to you, then trust your inner guidance to show you what is best for you. Seek the advice of appropriate professionals, and really listen to what they have to say. Take in feedback from friends and loved ones. Then listen deeply to your own sense of truth and make your own decisions about the best course of action.

Having done what you need to do to make sure your body is getting the care it requires, turn your attention to the other levels of your being. Find out what you need emotionally, mentally, and spiritually. Then take steps to care for those needs.

Remember that our bodies are wonderful communicators — they let us know what they need. Cultivate the art and practice of feeling, sensing, and listening to what your body is saying.

The technique of creative visualization can be a very powerful way of supporting healing and maintaining health, and can be used in combination with any other treatment modality. Since writing *Creative Visualization* in 1978, I have received thousands of letters from people who have used it successfully with almost every kind of physical ailment, as well as many other aspects of life.

~~~

Living in the Physical World

As we develop a healthy awareness of and respect for our own bodies, we gain greater awareness of the physical world around us. In addition to being sensitive to ourselves, we become sensitive to others and our environment. In caring for ourselves, we desire to care for our surroundings. When we respect and honor the physical plane, we create order, balance, and beauty around us.

Just as my body is the manifestation of my individual consciousness, the earth is our collective body, the manifestation of our collective consciousness. How we treat the earth is a reflection of how we treat ourselves. In order to thrive in the physical world we need to have an attitude of respect for it.

Mother Earth is our greatest teacher. If we pay attention, we can learn from her everything we need to know about living on the physical plane. Every day, in every way, she demonstrates to us her natural rhythms and cycles — all the natural laws of life.

Most of the indigenous cultures of the world had a deep understanding and reverence for humanity's connection with the earth. Their belief systems were built around the essential connections between our Mother Earth and our physical, emotional, mental, and spiritual well-being, both collectively and individually. The current resurgence of interest in the wisdom of indigenous peoples reflects a recognition that we have a great deal to learn from them about creating healthy relationships with ourselves, each other, and the earth.

The pressures of modern life tend to move us further and further from the natural cycles of the earth. We get up when the alarm clock rings; we go to bed after the 11 o'clock news. Life is structured according to what we *think* needs to be done, not according to our sensitivity to a natural rhythm. Yet, separated though we may be, we are still part of the earth. We need to acknowledge that, to respect the earth's rhythms and live in accordance with them.

We are not machines that can produce the same output each and every day, endlessly. Our mental and emotional states are different on sunny summer days than on cloudy winter days. And there are myriad other subtle changes throughout the day affecting us. If we can acknowledge and accept these differences each day, we can move more within the flow of life.

In order to get more in touch with our Earth connections, it is essential to be outside a little every day, even if it is just for a few minutes. It is only by having direct contact with the natural world that we can become conscious of the subtle changes occurring throughout the year. If you live in the city, it's a little more difficult to stay in touch with nature, but almost anyone can walk outside, observe the sky, and feel the sun and the air.

Daily physical movement is an important part of maintaining a healthy, happy body and soul. As we move our bodies, the life force can flow freely through, healing and replenishing our physical form and bringing us pleasure and joy.

An important part of developing the physical aspect of our being is cultivating the ability to successfully handle the practical aspects of living in the material world. We need to develop the skills that allow us to make a living, manage our money, maintain a clean and orderly household, organize our time, keep commitments, and generally show up and be accountable to ourselves and others. The ability to do these things is an indication of a developed consciousness in the physical realm.

There are many people in this world who are highly developed spiritually, mentally, and emotionally, but have denied the importance of the physical level. They often have a difficult time developing a successful career, earning money, or handling their finances appropriately. Often, their surroundings are chaotic, or they are somewhat spaced out, having trouble keeping agreements or appointments.

If you have trouble making a living or succeeding in the world, look to see if you have unconscious negative beliefs or feelings about physical existence. For example, if you have suffered a lot of emotional or physical pain you may deeply believe that life on earth is a painful place, where you can't get your needs met. Or if you were brought up in a traditional transcendent religion, you may still hold a core belief that the physical is less important than the spiritual. Perhaps you are reacting in rebellion against an upbringing that over-emphasized the importance of order and success on the material plane. Bringing these attitudes to consciousness allows them to heal and transform into respect and appreciation for physical life. Our physical, emotional, mental, and spiritual well-being depends on our ability to take care of ourselves and interact successfully with the world around us.

Exercise: Communicating with Your Body

Here is a meditation that can help you communicate with your physical body. Read through the whole meditation before you begin to practice.

Start by getting in a comfortable position either sitting or lying down, close your eyes, and relax.

Become aware of your thoughts and notice them as they parade through your mind. See if you can become aware of each thought as it moves through your mind, then consciously let it go. When the next thought comes, notice it, then let it go too.

Take a few deep breaths and as you exhale, relax your mind, and let it begin to slow down. On each exhale relax your entire body, continue to breathe deeply and slowly, and let your body become more and more relaxed.

Let your awareness begin to scan your body, starting with your feet. Contract your toes and feet, hold for a few seconds, then relax them. Feel them sink deeper into whatever you are sitting on or lying on. Next contract your calves, hold for a few seconds and release. After each release let your body sink deeper into whatever is holding you up. Continue this contract and release process up your entire body — thighs, pelvis, hips, abdomen, chest, hands, arms, shoulders, neck, head, and face. Contract each body part for a few seconds, release it, and let it sink into your support a bit deeper.

Now let your mind follow your breath, feeling each inhale fill your lungs and each exhale relax them. Notice the pause at the bottom of each exhale.

Let your awareness move through your body, and get in touch with a part of your body that needs your attention, for whatever reason — because it's in pain, it isn't functioning properly, or perhaps because it's tired. It might be a part of your body that doesn't feel accepted by you or by others.

Put one or both of your hands on that part of your body and put your full attention there. Ask that part of your body what it feels, needs, or what it wants to tell you. Listen or sense what it is feeling.

Imagine that your body is talking to you. What is it saying? Notice what is happening in your hands as they rest on your body.

Now, if it feels right, imagine loving, healing energy is coming from a pure source deep inside of you and flowing through your hands into that part of your body.

You could imagine it as a beautiful, warm, golden light or any color light that feels like what that part of your body needs. Send acceptance, love, and healing to that part.

Imagine this healing energy gently dissolving pain, tension, illness, and all lack of self love. Imagine your hands bringing fresh energy and vitality to your body.

Now imagine your whole body healthy, fit, beautiful, and filled with energy.

When you are ready, slowly lift your hands off your body, gently stretch, and gradually open your eyes and bring your consciousness back into the room.

If you wish, write down what you have experienced.

~

CHAPTER 6

INTEGRATION
AND
BALANCE

You may have noticed that the chapters in this book increased in length as we moved from the spiritual to the physical. This is because we are moving from learning to connect with the simple essence of who we are on the deepest level, to the complex task of learning to bring *all* aspects of who we are into living successfully in the physical realm.

This is truly a lifelong task — the great adventure of existence. Rather than approaching the four levels of healing as a goal to be reached as quickly as possible so we achieve some ideal state of balance, we need to understand that this is an ongoing, ever-unfolding journey. We need to have great patience, compassion, and acceptance of ourselves in the process.

As I stress throughout this book, there is no right way to do this; in fact, each person has his or her own unique path. Although others can serve as mentors and guides along the way, no one has all the answers for us. Fortunately, life itself is our best teacher; it always seems to lead or nudge us in the direction we need to go. And if we learn to pay attention, our own inner, intuitive guidance will show us each step we need to take along the way.

As we follow our healing path, giving our attention to each of the levels as the need arises, we find that all four aspects — spiritual, mental, emotional, and physical — gradually become more integrated with one another. Our lives increasingly come into greater balance and harmony.

In this book, I have offered a few exercises that may be helpful in healing each of the levels. If these exercises work for you, they can be used regularly as a program for developing and balancing all the aspects.

We are fortunate to live in a time in which there are so many tools for personal growth available to us. There are a seemingly infinite number of books, classes, workshops, groups, individual counselors, healers, and practitioners of various kinds, all offering an exciting and sometimes bewildering array of possibilities for our healing and growth. It's easy to get confused about what path to follow.

My best advice to those who may be trying to sort this out is this: Try to follow your intuitive sense — your gut feeling about what is right for you. If you feel drawn to a certain mode of personal growth, check it out, explore it, see if it seems to really benefit you. Stay with it as long as it clearly benefits you, and be willing to move on when it no longer does.

Beware of powerful charismatic leaders, gurus, or therapists whose followers or clients seem overly dependent and stay around them for many years. Trust your gut feelings if anything doesn't feel right, no matter how well it may be rationalized. Look for teachers and guides who clearly support their students or clients in becoming empowered and moving on with their lives.

There are many tools such as journaling, writing with your nondominant hand, and working with your dreams (learning to understand and interpret what they mean to you, not accepting someone else's ready-made interpretation of what certain symbols mean) that can help you use your daily life as your path of healing and growth.

On my own journey, I have learned and used many different tools and techniques at various times, and each one has helped me heal or develop a certain part of me. For example, creative visualization is a powerful tool (or more accurately, a set of tools) that can be used to bring healing to any or all of the four levels. As I mentioned earlier, learning to follow my intuitive inner guidance has been one of the most important practices in my life. For more information about these techniques, please refer to my books and tapes in the Recommended Resources section.

There is one method that has helped me more than any other with integrating the many aspects of myself and bringing my life into greater balance: the work of Drs. Hal and Sidra Stone, which I mentioned in an earlier chapter. They have developed the Psychology of Selves and a technique called Voice Dialogue, which is an extremely powerful way of getting in touch with and expressing the many selves we all have within us. In order to fully experience Voice Dialogue, it's necessary to work with a trained facilitator in a one-on-one session. However, a great deal of awareness and healing can be gained just by reading the Stones' books or listening to their tapes, which are listed in the Recommended Resources section. (Their tapes on dreams are an excellent way to learn about the dream process as well.) I have also included information on how to learn about their workshops. If you write or call their office, you can find out if there are Voice Dialogue facilitators in your area.

I lead workshops all over the world on the subject of the four levels of healing, as well as many other topics. Also, I conduct week-long intensives regularly in California and Hawaii, and occasionally in other areas, aimed at healing, developing, and balancing the four levels. In these intensives we use meditation, visualization, developing intuition, Voice Dialogue, writing, movement, art, dreams, and many other methods.

Exercise: Integration Meditation

Here is a meditation to help you integrate all four levels. This is a good one to do on a daily or regular basis.

Sit or lie down in a comfortable position with your back straight and supported. Close your eyes and relax. Take a deep breath, and as you exhale, let go of everything you don't need to focus on right now. Take another deep breath, and as you exhale, let your awareness move deep inside. Keep breathing slowly and fully, and allow your attention to move deeper and deeper inside. Move deeper than your body, mind, or emotions, until you come to a quiet place inside.

In this quiet place, open to feeling and experiencing your spiritual essence. Just sit quietly and invite your spirit in. Whether or not you feel anything in particular, just assume it's there. Know that it is always with you at every moment of your life. In this place, you are one with all of creation.

Now move slowly to the mental level. Imagine yourself very mentally clear and alert. Imagine that you believe in yourself, you have confidence in your power to create and manifest whatever you truly want in your life. You believe that life is supporting you in every way.

Now check in with yourself on the emotional level. How are you feeling right now? Can you accept and be with your feelings? Imagine yourself feeling comfortable with all your emotions. Know that as human beings we have many deep feelings that are gifts to help us take care of ourselves, to teach us about life. So imagine yourself respecting and honoring all your feelings and learning to express them appropriately and constructively.

Become aware of your physical body, and begin to sense how it feels. Give your body the love and appreciation it needs and deserves. Imagine that you are learning to listen to your body and pay attention to what it needs and feels. You take good care of it, and as a result it feels healthy, fit, alive, and beautiful. Imagine feeling comfortable and happy in your body.

Now expand that feeling to your surroundings. Imagine yourself feeling comfortable and confident in the physical world, able to take good care of yourself and handle the practical aspects of life easily and efficiently. Your environment reflects this — it is orderly and beautiful. Take a few minutes to

imagine your day unfolding in a flowing and fulfilling way.

When you feel complete with this, slowly open
your eyes, stretch gently, and go about your life.

Have a wonderful journey!

RECOMMENDED RESOURCES

Books

Bennett, Hal Zina. *Write from the Heart: Unleashing the Power of Your Creativity.* (Nataraj Publishing, Mill Valley, CA: 1995.)

Bodine, Echo. *Passion to Heal: The Ultimate Guide to Your Healing Journey.* (Nataraj Publishing, Mill Valley, CA: 1993.)

Cameron, Julia. *The Artist's Way: A Spiritual Path to Higher Creativity.* (Tarcher/Putnam, New York: 1992.)

Capacchione, Lucia. *The Power of Your Other Hand: A Course in Channeling the Inner Wisdom of the Right Brain.* (Newcastle Publishing Co., North Hollywood, CA: 1988.)

Capacchione, Lucia. *Recovery of Your Inner Child.* (Simon and Schuster, New York: 1991.)

Cassou, Michelle and Stewart Cubley. *Life, Paint and Passion: Reclaiming the Magic of Spontaneous Expression.* (Tarcher/Putnam, New York: 1995.)

Dossey, Larry, M.D. *Prayer Is Good Medicine:.* (HarperSan Francisco, CA: 1996.)

Gardener, Howard. *Frames of Mind: Theory of Multiple Intelligences.* (Basic Books, New York: 1983.)

Gawain, Shakti. *Creative Visualization,* (Nataraj/New World Library, Novato, CA: 1978.)

Gawain, Shakti (with Laurel King). *Living in the Light: A Guide to Personal and Planetary Transformation.* (Nataraj/New World Library, Novato, CA: 1986.)

Gawain, Shakti. *Return to the Garden: A Journey of Discovery.* (Nataraj/New World Library, Novato, CA: 1993.)

Gawain, Shakti. *Awakening: A Daily Guide to Conscious Living.* (Nataraj/New World Library, Novato, CA: 1991.)

Gawain, Shakti. *The Path of Transformation: How Healing Ourselves Can Change the World.* (Nataraj/New World Library, Novato, CA: 1993.)

Metzger, Deena. *Writing for Your Life: A Guide and Companion to the Inner Worlds.* (HarperSanFrancisco, San Francisco, CA: 1992.)

Myss, Carolyn. *Anatomy of the Spirit: 7 Stages of Power and Healing.* (Harmony Books, New York: 1996.)

Nelson, Martia. *Coming Home: The Return to True Self.* (Nataraj/New World Library, Novato, CA: 1993.)

Northrup, Christiane, M.D. *Women's Bodies, Women's Wisdom: Creating Physical and Emotional Health and Healing.* (Bantam Books, New York: 1994.) For information about her newsletter call "Woman to Woman" at (207) 846-6163.

Roth, Gabrielle. *Maps to Ecstasy: Teachings of an Urban*

Shaman. (Nataraj/New World Library, Novato, CA: 1993.)

Stone, Hal, M.D. and Sidra Stone, M.D. *Embracing Our Selves: The Voice Dialogue Manual*. (Nataraj/New World Library, Novato, CA: 1989.)

Stone, Hal, M.D. and Sidra Stone, M.D. *Embracing Each Other: Relationship as Teacher, Healer, and Guide*. (Nataraj/New World Library, Novato, CA: 1989.)

Stone, Hal, M.D. and Sidra Stone, M.D. *Embracing Your Inner Critic: Turning Self-Criticism into a Creative Asset*. (HarperSanFrancisco, San Francisco, CA: 1993.)

Stone, Sidra. *The Shadow King: The Invisible Force That Holds Women Back*. (Nataraj/New World Library, Novato, CA: 1997.)

Weil, Andrew, M.D. *Spontaneous Healing: How to Discover and Enhance Your Body's Natural Ability to Maintain and Heal Itself*. (Knopf, New York: 1995.)

$\sim$

Audiotapes

Gawain, Shakti: Teaching and meditation audiotapes published by Nataraj/New World Library, Novato, CA.

> *The Four Levels of Healing: A Guide to Balancing the Spiritual, Mental, Emotional, and Physical Aspects of Life.*
>
> *Living in the Light: Book on Tape.* Abridged version.
>
> *The Path of Transformation: Book on Tape.* Abridged version.
>
> *Developing Intuition.*
>
> *Creative Visualization.*
>
> *Meditations.*

Roth, Gabrielle: Music audiotapes to move to, published by Raven Recordings, NJ.

> *Initiation.*
>
> *Totem.*
>
> *Endless Wave: Volume One.*
>
> *Refuge.*

Stone, Hal, M.D., and Sidra Stone, M.D.: Teaching audiotapes, published by Delos, Albion, CA.

> *Meeting Your Selves.*
>
> *The Child Within.*
>
> *Meet Your Inner Critic.*
>
> *Meet Your Inner Critic II.*
>
> *Meet the Pusher.*
>
> *The Dance of Selves in Relationship.*

Understanding Your Relationships.
Decoding Your Dreams.
Exploring the Dark Side in Dreams.
Our Lost Instinctual Heritage.

Videotapes

Gawain, Shakti:*The Path of Transformation.* Videotape of live talk. (Hay House, Inc., Carlsbad, CA: 1992.)

Roth, Gabrielle. *Ecstatic Dance: A Workout for Body and Soul.* Movement video. (Raven Recordings, NJ: 1993.)

WORKSHOPS

Shakti Gawain leads workshops all over the United States and in many other countries. She also conducts retreats, intensives, and training programs. If you would like to be on her mailing list and receive workshop information, contact:

Shakti Gawain, Inc.
P.O. Box 377, Mill Valley, CA 94942
Telephone: (415) 388-7140
Fax: (415) 388-7196
e-mail: sg@nataraj.com

Shakti and her husband, Jim Burns, rent rooms and a guest cottage at their beautiful estate on the Hawaiian island of Kauai, for individuals and couples wishing to come for personal retreats. Shakti also conducts week-long intensives on Kauai. For information or to make reservations, contact:

Kai Mana
P.O. Box 612, Kilauea, Hawaii 96754
Telephone: (808) 828-1280 or (800) 837-1782
Fax: (808) 828-6670

For information about Shakti's workshops,
Nataraj Publishing, and Kai Mana
check out our web site at:
http://www.shaktigawain.com

For information about Drs. Hal and Sidra Stone's workshops and trainings, contact:

Delos
P.O. Box 604, Albion, CA 95410
Telephone: (707) 937-2424
E-mail: delos@mcn.org
or see the website at:
http://www.delos-inc.com

For information about Gabrielle Roth's workshops, contact:

Raven Recording
P.O. Box 2034, Red Bank, NJ 07701
Telephone:1(800)76-RAVEN

About the Author

Shakti Gawain is the bestselling author of *Creative Visualization, Living in the Light, Return to the Garden, The Path of Transformation,* and several other books. A warm, articulate, and inspiring teacher, Shakti leads workshops internationally. For more than twenty years, she has facilitated thousands of people in learning to trust and act on their own inner truth, thus releasing and developing their creativity in every aspect of their lives.

Shakti and her husband, Jim Burns, make their home in Mill Valley, California and on the island of Kauai.